Getting Started in French for Kids

A Children's Learn French Books

BABY PROFESSOR
EDUCATION KIDS

Speedy Publishing LLC
40 E. Main St. #1156
Newark, DE 19711
www.speedypublishing.com

Let's learn some of the common French words.

FRENCH	ENGLISH
c'est	**that's**
/sɛ/	

Trace the word.

c'est   c'est   c'est

Rewrite the word.

FRENCH	ENGLISH
voilà	**are**
/vwala/	

Trace the word.

voilà   voilà   voilà

Rewrite the word.

FRENCH	ENGLISH
et	and
/e/	

Trace the word.

et   et   et

Rewrite the word.

FRENCH	ENGLISH
mais	but
/mɛ/	

Trace the word.

mais   mais   mais

Rewrite the word.

FRENCH	ENGLISH

maintenant

/mɛ̃tnɑ̃/

now

Trace the word.

maintenant   maintenant

Rewrite the word.

FRENCH	ENGLISH

surtout

/syʀtu/

especially

Trace the word.

surtout   surtout   surtout

Rewrite the word.

FRENCH	ENGLISH
sauf	**except**

/sof/

Trace the word.

sauf   sauf   sauf

Rewrite the word.

FRENCH	ENGLISH
bien sûr	**of course**

/bjɛ̃ syʀ/

Trace the word.

bien sûr   bien sûr   bien sûr

Rewrite the word.

FRENCH	ENGLISH
pas mal	not bad
/pa mal/	

Trace the word.

pas mal pas mal pas mal

Rewrite the word.

FRENCH	ENGLISH
le livre	book
/lə livʀ/	

Trace the word.

le livre le livre le livre

Rewrite the word.

FRENCH	ENGLISH
le crayon	**pencil**
/lə kʀɛjɔ̃/	

Trace the word.

le crayon   le crayon

Rewrite the word.

- -

FRENCH	ENGLISH
le stylo	**pen**
/lə stilo/	

Trace the word.

le stylo   le stylo   le stylo

Rewrite the word.

FRENCH	ENGLISH

le papier

/lə papje/

paper

Trace the word.

le papier le papier

Rewrite the word.

FRENCH	ENGLISH

le chien

/lə ʃjɛ̃/

dog

Trace the word.

le chien le chien le chien

Rewrite the word.

FRENCH	ENGLISH
le chat	cat
/lə ʃa/	

Trace the word.

le chat   le chat   le chat

Rewrite the word.

FRENCH	ENGLISH
l'argent (m)	money
/laʀʒã/	

Trace the word.

l'argent (m)   l'argent (m)

Rewrite the word.

FRENCH	ENGLISH
toujours	always
/tuʒuʀ/	

Trace the word.

toujours   toujours   toujours

Rewrite the word.

FRENCH	ENGLISH
souvent	often
/suvã/	

Trace the word.

souvent   souvent   souvent

Rewrite the word.

FRENCH	ENGLISH
quelquefois	sometimes
/kɛlkəfwa/	

Trace the word.

quelquefois   quelquefois

Rewrite the word.

FRENCH	ENGLISH
d'habitude	usually
/dabityd/	

Trace the word.

d'habitude   d'habitude

Rewrite the word.

FRENCH	ENGLISH
aussi	also
/osi/	

Trace the word.

aussi   aussi   aussi

Rewrite the word.

- -

FRENCH	ENGLISH
encore	again
/ã kɔʀ/	

Trace the word.

encore   encore   encore

Rewrite the word.

FRENCH	ENGLISH
en retard	late
/ãʀətaʀ/	

Trace the word.

en retard   en retard

Rewrite the word.

FRENCH	ENGLISH
presque	almost
/pʀɛsk/	

Trace the word.

presque   presque   presque

Rewrite the word.

FRENCH	ENGLISH
une amie	friend
/y nami/	

Trace the word.

une amie une amie une amie

Rewrite the word.

FRENCH	ENGLISH
une femme	woman
/yn fam/	

Trace the word.

une femme une femme

Rewrite the word.

FRENCH	ENGLISH

un homme

/œ̃ nɔm/

man

Trace the word.

un homme   un homme

Rewrite the word.

FRENCH	ENGLISH

une fille

/yn fij/

girl

Trace the word.

une fille   une fille   une fille

Rewrite the word.

FRENCH	ENGLISH
un garçon	boy
/œ̃ gaʁsɔ̃/	

Trace the word.

un garçon   un garçon

Rewrite the word.

FRENCH	ENGLISH
le travail	work
/lə tʁavaj/	

Trace the word.

le travail   le travail

Rewrite the word.

FRENCH	ENGLISH
lundi	**Monday**
lundi */luhN-dee/*	

Trace the word.

lundi   lundi   lundi

Rewrite the word.

FRENCH	ENGLISH
mardi	**Tuesday**
/mahr-dee/	

Trace the word.

mardi   mardi   mardi

Rewrite the word.

FRENCH	ENGLISH
mercredi	Wednesday
/mehr-kruh-dee/	

Trace the word.

mercredi mercredi mercredi

Rewrite the word.

FRENCH	ENGLISH
jeudi	Thursday
/zhuh-dee/	

Trace the word.

jeudi   jeudi   jeudi

Rewrite the word.

FRENCH	ENGLISH
vendredi	Friday

/vahN-druh-dee/

Trace the word.

vendredi   vendredi   vendredi

Rewrite the word.

FRENCH	ENGLISH
samedi	Saturday

/sahm-dee/

Trace the word.

samedi   samedi   samedi

Rewrite the word.

FRENCH	ENGLISH
dimanche	**Sunday**
/dee-mahNsh/	

Trace the word.

dimanche   dimanche

Rewrite the word.

FRENCH	ENGLISH
elle	**she**
/ɛl/	

Trace the word.

elle   elle   elle

Rewrite the word.

FRENCH	ENGLISH
nous	**we**
/nu/	

Trace the word.

nous   nous   nous

Rewrite the word.

FRENCH	ENGLISH
vous	**you**
/vu/	

Trace the word.

vous   vous   vous

Rewrite the word.

Let's learn some of the common French numbers.

FRENCH	ENGLISH
Un	One
/œ̃ /	

Trace the word.

Un   Un   Un

Rewrite the word.

FRENCH	ENGLISH
Deux	Two
/dø/	

Trace the word.

Deux   Deux   Deux

Rewrite the word.

FRENCH	ENGLISH
Trois	**Three**
/trwa/	

Trace the word.

Trois   Trois

Rewrite the word.

FRENCH	ENGLISH
Quatre	**Four**
/katr/	

Trace the word.

Quatre   Quatre   Quatre

Rewrite the word.

FRENCH	ENGLISH
Cinq	Five

/sɛ̃k/

Trace the word.

Cinq   Cinq   Cinq

Rewrite the word.

FRENCH	ENGLISH
Six	Six

/sis/

Trace the word.

Six   Six   Six

Rewrite the word.

FRENCH	ENGLISH
Sept	Seven
/sɛt/	

Trace the word.

Sept   Sept

Rewrite the word.

FRENCH	ENGLISH
Huit	Eight
/ˈɥit/	

Trace the word.

Huit   Huit   Huit

Rewrite the word.

FRENCH	ENGLISH
Neuf	Nine

/nœf/

Trace the word.

Neuf   Neuf   Neuf

Rewrite the word.

FRENCH	ENGLISH
Dix	Ten

/dis/

Trace the word.

Dix   Dix   Dix

Rewrite the word.

Let's learn French colors.

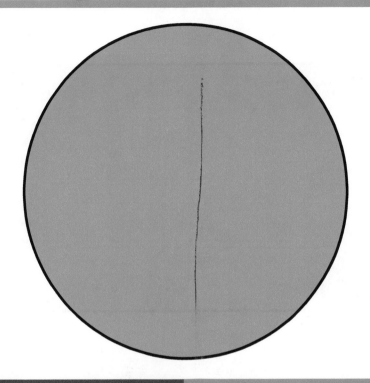

FRENCH	ENGLISH
rouge	red

/RUƷ/

Trace the word.

rouge   rouge

Rewrite the word.

FRENCH	ENGLISH
orange	orange

/ɔʀɑ̃ʒ/

Trace the word.

orange   orange

Rewrite the word.

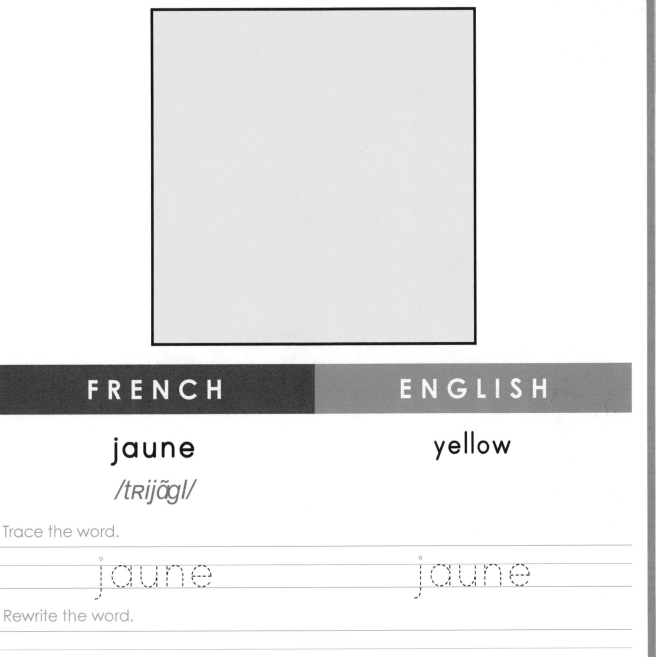

FRENCH	ENGLISH
jaune	**yellow**
/tʀɪjãgl/	

Trace the word.

jaune   jaune

Rewrite the word.

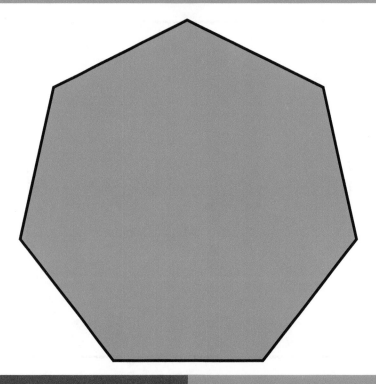

FRENCH	ENGLISH
verte	**green**
/vɛʀt/	

Trace the word.

verte   verte

Rewrite the word.

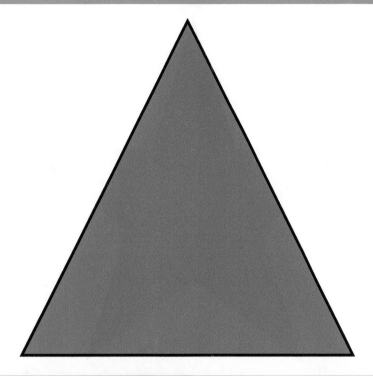

FRENCH	ENGLISH
bleue	**blue**
/blø/	

Trace the word.

bleue   bleue

Rewrite the word.

FRENCH	ENGLISH
violette	**purple**
/vjɔlɛt/	

Trace the word.

violette   *violette*

Rewrite the word.

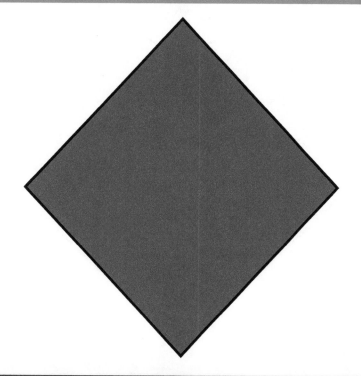

FRENCH	ENGLISH
brune	**brown**
/bʀyn/	

Trace the word.

brune   brune

Rewrite the word.

FRENCH	ENGLISH
rose	**pink**
/ROZ/	

Trace the word.

rose   rose

Rewrite the word.

FRENCH	ENGLISH
noire	**black**
/nwaʀ/	

Trace the word.

noire noire

Rewrite the word.

Visit

BABY PROFESSOR
EDUCATION KIDS

www.BabyProfessorBooks.com

to download Free Baby Professor eBooks
and view our catalog of new and exciting
Children's Books

CPSIA information can be obtained
at www.ICGtesting.com
Printed in the USA
BVHW012020071121
621020BV00013B/607